MW00436550

Romantic
Conflict

The GOSPEL for REAL LIFE series

Brad Hambrick, Series Editor

Romantic Conflict

EMBRACING DESIRES THAT
BLESS NOT BRUISE

BRAD HAMBRICK

P&R
PUBLISHING
P.O. BOX 817 • PHILLIPSBURG • NEW JERSEY 08865-0817

Unless otherwise indicated, Scripture quotations are from *ESV Bible* ® (*The Holy Bible, English Standard Version* ®). Copyright © 2001 by Crossway Bibles, a publishing ministry of Good News Publishers. Used by permission. All rights reserved.

Italics within Scripture quotations indicate emphasis added.

ISBN: 978-1-59638-998-4 (pbk)
ISBN: 978-1-59638-999-1 (ePub)
ISBN: 978-1-59638-348-7 (Mobi)

Printed in the United States of America

WHEN MANY COUPLES BEGIN to rehearse their arguments or their requests for romance, they begin to hear very familiar patterns. The following poem captures the rise and fall of common marital disagreements in the form of a Dr. Seuss book. Note the innocent beginning, rise to desperation, and bewildered conclusion.

My name is Sam;
A good spouse I am.
Simple needs are all I ask.
Not too hard is any task.
Listen, touch me, hold my hand;
Let's go for a walk on the sand.

I would kiss you on the mouth,
But please not outside the house.
Time together, just name the place,
But after everything is in its space.
I've done so much—you know it's true—
How could you doubt that I love you?

It feels like I give more than I receive;
Neglect is all that I can perceive.
Anyone fairly keeping score
Would clearly see that I've done more.
The omitted things that I have asked
Reveal you want this marriage axed.

I do not want to bring this pain.
Why make me ask these things again?
A happy marriage should not depend
On how well I can pretend.

If you cannot be my friend,
We should just call this the end.

I hate you; I love you—
Can both really be true?
Don't leave me; get out of my face—
How can we share this same space?
Things can be so good, so bad;
Our marriage may just drive me mad.

We'll stay together for the kids,
But I refuse to live on the skids.
What's the point? We're both unhappy.
"Happily ever after" now seems so sappy.
If this is what God designed,
Should we really just live resigned?

When I take the time to think it through,
I remember the things I love about you.
Differences that seemed monumental
Suddenly seem much more trivial.
How will we ever be free
To enjoy marriage as God meant it to be?

How will we be able to enjoy the blessings God intended to provide through marriage without becoming consumed by our desire for them? Few marriages fall apart because of evil desires. Few embittered spouses seem crazy for wanting the things that have been neglected. But equally true is the reality that the good desires of well-meaning spouses will not always get along.

- The innocent desires of the introvert and the extrovert will clash even when no one is sinning.
- The desires of a spender and a saver, even when each is within the constraints of wisdom, will often clash.

- A "pleasant evening" will be different for someone who values time together than for someone who values productivity.

In a broken world with limited time and money, not every legitimate desire can be fulfilled. Often fulfilling one person's desire results in neglecting another person's. Unfortunately, we tend to quickly forget our blessings and long remember our sufferings. Our unmet desires bark louder than our fulfilled desires cheer.

- We remember a few harsh words better than many pleasant words.
- An omitted "Thank you" can speak louder in our emotions than many spoken expressions of gratitude.
- A well-spoken "Not tonight" can easily feel like "We never will."

What we can say, with the clarity and pungency of a Dr. Seuss rhyme, is that often our hurts and disappointments may be real (authentic to our experience) but not true (accurately representing the situation). But things we tell ourselves persuasively and repeat to ourselves often become as real to us as "green eggs and ham" even if the result is marital food poisoning.

It may be surprising to many that Jesus' foundational call to be a disciple addressed this very issue: how do we enjoy the good things God gives to us without becoming consumed by our desire for them (or by their momentary absence, or by their not arriving in our preferred style)?

These good things that God intends to provide through marriage exist at the intersection of conflict and romance. As we consider this essential intersection within married life, we will examine one primary passage: Luke 9:23–24.

And he said to all, "If anyone would come after me, let him deny himself and take up his cross daily and follow me. For whoever would save his life will lose it, but whoever loses his life for my sake will save it."

In the course of this booklet we will go through this passage three times. First, we will walk through the straightforward application of the passage. Second, we will use the key principles of this passage to rewrite how we do conflict. Third, we will allow this passage to reignite romance within our marriages.

The goal is more than to apply principles from Scripture to hard situations. Rather, our goal is to use Scripture as the lens by which we see ourselves, our spouses, our marriages, and our difficult moments of powerful change (for better or worse). As you read, be prepared for how vividly even two verses of Scripture can capture, reframe, and transform the most mundane, the most personal, and the most challenging moments of life.

TAKE ONE: THE SIMPLE MEANING OF THE PASSAGE

This is a painfully simple passage with a profoundly counterintuitive twist at the end. We will briefly look at eight points within these two verses in order to set the stage for "Take Two: Conflict" and "Take Three: Romance."

"To all . . . If anyone . . ." No one is exempt from this passage. Some passages of Scripture have a relatively narrow primary audience—husbands, wives, children, pastors, workers, singles, and so on. But that is not the case here. Based upon the words "all" and "anyone" there is only one category of people who can be exempt from this teaching: those who willfully reject Christ. Yet, as we will see, even those who choose not to follow Christ cannot escape the relational and emotional dynamics described in this passage.

"Come after . . . follow me". There is no such thing as a good, married Christian who is a bad spouse. A premise of this booklet is that a good Christ-follower is, by definition, a good spouse-lover. Anyone who is marked by the fruit of the Spirit (Gal. 5:22–23), addresses her own faults before lovingly confronting others (Matt. 7:3–5), and puts the interest of others ahead of her own (Phil. 2:1–11) will be a great spouse. We must resist the tendency to treat marriage enrichment as if it were unrelated to the character transformation that occurs in basic discipleship.

"Deny himself". The biggest obstacle to being a great spouse stares at each of us from the mirror every morning. Too often we become distracted and consumed by the things we cannot change and we turn a blind eye to the focal point of God's primary work in our lives. A great marriage is hard for the same reason that the Christian life is hard: it requires us to deny ourselves and to accept by faith that change is needed and that God offers something better—in terms of quality, quantity, method, and sustainability—than our natural selves would pursue.

"Take up his cross daily". A good marriage and the Christian life are not only hard; they are work. They are not something that we achieved (past tense verb) but something we surrender to (present tense verb) daily. We do not get to take a break from being a Christian or a good spouse. We need to remind ourselves continually that this work (daily denying self) is done in Christ's strength, not ours, and that it is his performance and righteousness, not ours, that make us acceptable to God. The defining mark of both a Christian and a good spouse is willingness to learn to enjoy the daily transformation involved in each.

"Life". This is *the* big question: "Where do you find life?" What gives you life? Who do you turn to in order to get life? We will come back to this question in "Take Two: Conflict"

and "Take Three: Romance." So pause now and begin to consider your answer.

- Where do you turn for relief after a stressful day?
- On what do you cast your cares when life is hard?
- What is your reward when you've done well?
- How do you most frequently complete your "if only . . ." daydreams?

The answer to these questions will be the center of your marital conflict and romance and of your walk with Christ.

"Save . . . lose". Jesus says that most of what we do to control the things that matter most to us winds up making life worse. We are like Wile E. Coyote trying out one Acme product after another to catch the Road Runner. Every time, we get blown up or wind up falling off a cliff in the process. As we continually try to squeeze hope, love, peace, and security out of this life with our "commonsense best practices," they inevitably slip through our fingers and we end up with pain, fear, despair, and insecurity. The result is that we try harder (become controlling, for example), give up (become neglectful), distract ourselves (overspend), shrink our world (obsess), or find some other way to "save our lives" that hurts our marriages.

"Lose . . . save". This is the essence of faith in the gospel. It is the painful part of giving up nothing to get everything. We must be willing to surrender those things that can only temporarily satisfy (at best) in order to receive eternal satisfaction (God himself). After this exchange we realize two things. First, that "life" (hope, righteousness, security) was the very thing keeping us from God. Second, that we can now enjoy those things we previously tried to squeeze life from because they are now placed in proportion. In hindsight this

is a trade we would label a "no-brainer." In the moment it is always frightening.

"For my sake". The gospel is not a gimmick or a game. The gospel is not a set of rules by which we can manipulate God and get him to give us what we really want. If we do not ultimately want God, then we do not get the gospel and will not be able to enjoy anything else (at least not for long). Too often we come to God asking for a loan instead of an inheritance. We're asking for the right things on the basis of the wrong relationship (as peasants instead of children). When we allow the gospel to transform who we are and why we live, then we will ask for the same kinds of things others ask for (including a good marriage) but for different reasons and with different expectations.

Hopefully you are already beginning to hear echoes of what goes wrong in your marital conflict and of what you want to go right in your marital romance. But let's transition into our second walk through this passage as we delve into the subject of conflict.

TAKE TWO: CONFLICT REWRITTEN

On our first walk through this passage we went phrase by phrase through Jesus' teaching. This time we are going to take a narrative approach. The narrative we'll walk through is that of a typical conflict in your home. We'll introduce ways to structure and interrupt these typical conflicts with the core lessons in Luke 9:23–24.

To begin this section, start by remembering the last several arguments you've had with your spouse. If you're like the vast majority of couples, you don't have hundreds of different arguments. You have the same handful of arguments with dozens of different triggers and details.

Make a few notes about these arguments in order to help
you read your life into the material that follows.

_____

_____

_____

_____

In order to help you learn this material, I suggest that you
imagine one or more of these arguments occurring at your kitchen
table, which we'll decorate with various trinkets as we go through
this section. In the next section I'll redesign your bedroom.
(I openly admit to being one of those "intrusive counselors"!)

Even if you don't actually get a box full of trinkets out on the
kitchen table, if you take the imagery seriously, it will help you
to visualize how the gospel transforms conflict and will never
allow you to see conflict the same way again. Part of our objec-
tive is to ruin conflict for you. Too often we are too comfortable
with patterns that are too destructive. We need new eyes to see
ourselves if we are going to live differently (Ezek. 12:2).

Come to the Table

Start by sitting down at the table. If during an episode of
conflict either of you is unable to sit at a table with the other, you
do not have a relational problem—you have a personal problem.
Self-control is a fruit of the Spirit (Gal. 5:22–23) and not the
product of a relationship. If this describes your behavior, you
need to deal with your anger and quit thinking about what your
spouse is or is not doing. No "marital exercise" will compensate
for a personal character deficiency.

Next, each of you should hold a picture of both of you in
your hands—preferably a recent picture with the two of you
smiling. Holding this picture represents that you are valuing

the marriage more than whatever issue is being discussed and more than your desires that are impacted by the disagreement.

Then each of you should place objects that represent your most common or significant desires in front of you on the table. Again, most couples fight about the same things over and over again in different situations. These objects represent the things that you want badly enough that you are frequently willing to sin against your spouse in order to attain them.

The list below is meant to help you identify what these driving desires are (if the desires are a new concept for you or are hard for you to put into words) and provides examples of the kinds of objects you might put on the table. For the purposes of this exercise and the next, do not select any of these objects that would be offensive to your spouse. The suggestions are meant only to spark creativity, so please identify things that are very "you."

If trying to be creative annoys you or stresses you out, then just write the bold text words that represent the things that are most important to you on a piece of paper and put those on the table. But be patient with your spouse, who will likely want to have fun and be "meaningful" with this part of the exercise.

- **Acceptance:** the lyrics to the hymn "Just As I Am," a list of your insecurities, a picture of receiving a hug on a bad day
- **Respect:** a picture of a mutually trusted leader, glasses (to represent eye contact), a net (to represent trust), a piece of paper saying "I believe in you"
- **Power/Influence:** a megaphone (to represent having a voice), a piece of paper with the words *yes* and *no* written on it, a map (to represent choosing direction)
- **Benefit of Doubt:** a cup with "half full" written on it, a piece of paper saying "I believe you," a magnifying glass with a broken lens
- **Order/Predictability:** a day planner, a neatly folded towel, an organization flowchart, a GPS

- **Peace:** a picture of a desolate beach, a favorite relaxation object, the word *silence* written on a piece of paper
- **Freedom:** a "Get Out of Jail Free" card, an American flag, something representing your favorite guilty pleasure
- **Hobby:** a golf ball, an empty shotgun shell, a favorite Pinterest project
- **Being Understood:** a personal journal, a comic strip that captures who you are, the phrase "if you don't understand, ask more questions"
- **Support:** a few Jenga blocks, a "That Was Easy" button from Staples, a toy life preserver
- **Romance/Affection:** a heart-shaped pillow, two gloves placed hand in hand, the word *sex* written on a piece of paper (probably best not to be too creative with what you put on the table for this one)
- **Unity:** two candles (to represent the unity candle part of a wedding ceremony), two strings tied in a knot, an HP and Mac logo on the same piece of paper (I'm dreaming big with this one)
- **Ease/Fun/Comfort:** a television remote, a bookmark, a piece of paper saying "off duty," a blanket (à la Linus)
- **My Way:** a Frank Sinatra album, an ace of spades (as a trump card), a "One Way" street sign
- **Affirmation/Gratitude:** a thank you card, a drawing of a smile, a list of things you wouldn't change about your life or marriage
- **Rest:** a pillow, a favorite book, a favorite blend of coffee, an ergonomic wrist pillow
- **Fairness:** a referee whistle, old-fashioned balance scales, an apple and an orange
- **Dream Fulfilled:** if you don't know what to put here, this is an important conversation to have with yourself and with your spouse
- **Protection:** a hard hat, a shield, a padlock, an antivirus software box

You'll quickly notice something about this list. These are all good things. No reasonable person wants to do without any of them, and no healthy marriage is significantly deficient in these areas. This is what makes our bad actions in conflict feel so justified: most often we are vying for good things.

But before you move on, stop to evaluate whether some of the things you want have become good words with corrupted definitions. Too often *respect* can begin to mean "never being questioned," or *peace* can mean "never being asked to do anything uncomfortable." *Love* can mean "knowing what I'm thinking without my telling you." In these cases good words become wolves in sheep's clothing. We are being manipulative because we are labeling unrealistic expectations with nice words.

The goodness of the desires that lead to most conflicts is one of the most striking observations from James 4:1–2. When James asks, "What causes quarrels and what causes fights among you?" his answer is, "Your *passions* are at war within you. . . . You *desire* and do not have. . . . You *covet* and cannot obtain." If you study the words *passions*, *desire*, and *covet* in the original Greek you'll notice that two of the three are neutral (even positive) terms.

James is not rebuking these believers for what they want. He is correcting them for wanting good things so badly that they are willing to devour one another in order to obtain them. Notice this: when we demand the things we want, they become less satisfying and there is less unity when we get them. But James's readers were so blinded by the goodness of what they were pursuing that they wouldn't acknowledge this deterioration (nor will we).

- The more we demand respect, the less we can see or appreciate small acts of honor.
- The more we demand gratitude, the less we can sense common forms of appreciation.
- The more we insist on a particular expression of love, the more blind and deaf we become to other forms of love.

Instead we double down on our increasingly ineffective approach to "saving our lives." We become sin-blind. We see the world through the lens of the objects on the table. We hear everything our spouses say through the filter of whether it is appeasing the desires of our heart. We forget that we cannot truly have (i.e., enjoy) the things on the table until they no longer have us (i.e., keep us believing that we "need" them).

We realize (or at least we should realize) that these desires have become idols that are reinterpreting everything we experience. In a way we don't want to admit, we are living, moving, and having our being in our overgrown desires (contra Acts 17:28)—we have become children made in the image of our idolatrous desires instead of the image of our heavenly Father and Creator.

Notice that in these moments our desires begin to play every role that God should play—defining friend and foe, good and bad, what is worth our time and not worth our time, and so on. We "trust and obey" what our idolatrous desires say without question even if it means harming those we love most. We begin to follow our idols naturally, but when Christ calls us to follow him in the same way, we find it uncomfortable.

Pause for a moment and hear Luke 14:26 in light of this reality. Jesus said, "If anyone comes to me and does not hate his own father and mother and wife and children and brothers and sisters, yes, and even his own life, he cannot be my disciple." We cringe when we hear Jesus say this, but we blindly follow our desires into destructive conflict when they ask the same. But Jesus can be trusted in a way that our desires cannot.

This is what we must see if we are going to rescue our marital conflicts from becoming something that poisons our covenant with mistrust, scorekeeping, and bitterness. This will be a challenging process of denying ourselves and trusting that if we lose our lives (the objects on the table) we will actually save them (have something better). So let's see what comes next in the process.

See the Exchange

As you have your conflict and are sitting at the table holding your picture, if you communicate with dishonor, then you must put the picture down and pick up the object that you are valuing more than your marriage at that moment. This is the painful reality that James 4:1–2 and Luke 6:45 ("out of the abundance of the heart his mouth speaks") alert us to. Our words, even our careless ones (Matt. 12:34–37), reveal our true selves.

What does it look like to communicate with dishonor? To communicate with dishonor is to value something (an object, activity, or desire) more than someone (a relationship). Common examples of communicating with dishonor are raising your voice, using condescending tones, stringing together unanswerable rhetorical questions, giving the silent treatment, bringing up past offenses, calling names, exaggerating, changing subjects, telling your spouse what he was really thinking or why she did something (being a "mind reader"), shaming, being defensive about genuine faults, using passive-aggressive forms of appeasement, or creating emotional distance in other ways.

It might be easy to miss the significance of putting down the picture and picking up the object. This kind of action can easily become a mere acknowledgement that "I'm being bad" instead of a moment of genuine insight and conviction. This is what is happening every time we sin, either inside our marriages or outside them. We are putting down relationships (and ultimately our relationship with God) to pick up things we believe will give us more or better life.

Sin is not just the violation of a set of rules made by God. Sin is the expression of our primary allegiance and of what or who we value most. Too often we gloss over this reality with the biblically untenable phrase "You know I didn't mean that." What we should say is that we now, by God's grace, realize the foolishness of our sin and no longer want to be the kind of people who would trade our relationships for what we want.

Seeing the emptiness of this exchange is vital to genuine repentance that results in lasting change rooted in the gospel and that believes holiness is a blessing instead of a chore. Blindness to this exchange makes submission to godly communication seem like guilt-based coercion that always allows your spouse to "win."

If you take the step of putting down the picture and picking up the object, the next step in healthy, gospel-centered conflict will become very intuitive (although still not easy). Acknowledge your sin to your spouse, repent, put the object down, pick up the picture, and ask for the opportunity to continue the conversation.

This is the only way back to relational sanity. Until we do this we will continue to rationalize that sacrificing the marriage for one of our desires was the "only logical response" in each circumstance. But sin is never logical, and even if our spouses acquiesce to our demands, there will not be the kind of satisfaction, peace, and unity we hoped for when we picked up the objects of our desire.

This exercise should have another effect: it should show us how much we neglect what is important to our spouses during conflict. There are objects on both sides of the table, yet when we feel that our desires are threatened we become so shortsighted that we fail to see the things that are important to our spouses (except, perhaps, as competition to our own desires).

We must realize how much our untamed desires create the situation of a "pink team" and a "blue team," in which our differences are more significant than our covenant and only one "team" can "win." Let us never forget that, in marriage, if one person wins then both spouses lose. This is what it means to be "one flesh" (Gen. 2:24).

This doesn't mean that objects on both sides of the table ever will (or should) mirror one another. Marriage does not make us the same person, but it does make us one team. Our ability to be blind to the things that are most important to our spouses should humble us as we realize how easily we are mesmerized by the "deceitfulness of sin" (Heb. 3:13).

Live the Contradiction

Now we should be able to see more clearly how Jesus' conclusion in Luke 9:24 is true. If we seek to save our objects of desire we will lose them, or at least what we get will be an unsatisfying imitation of what we wanted.

- If we demand gratitude, we may hear "thank you," but it won't do for us what we wanted.
- If we demand affection, we may get a kiss, but it will not create the energy we desired.
- If we insist on quality time, we may be in the same room for a while, but the time will likely seem flat.
- If we insist on time to engage our hobbies, we will feel guilty as we do so and will grow in bitterness.
- If we insist on unity, we will wonder whether it is just appeasement and when "the other shoe is going to drop" as we try to get along.

Intuitively we know this, which is why we often wait until we are upset to ask for the things that are important to us. We'll address that dynamic in "Take Three: Romance." The inevitable disappointment dynamic is what causes so many couples to give up on their marriages, believing they have "irreconcilable differences." But that is just modern language for what happens when we try to "save our lives" with marriage and fail to submit our desires and marriages to God.

To see this, let's go back to the table. We have not finished our argument (how does that make you feel?). Visualize getting through your disagreement, putting down the picture each time a desire begins to rule your heart, then repentantly picking it up and asking to continue. What happens then? What is the "reward"?

The gospel blossoms in your marriage.

You can put down the picture again, but this time get up, walk to the other side of the table, pick up your spouse's objects, and say something like this: "You're not crazy for wanting these things. I want you to have these things. More than that, I want our marriage to be a safe place for us to pursue these things together. I don't want you to feel like you have to compete with me for these things; I am for you. Thank you for being willing to sacrifice these while we discussed [summarize subject], but I want you to have them."

Then your spouse can say something similar as he or she hands you the objects of your desire. While this may sound cheesy and foreign, pause for a moment and compare it to what you call "normal." In a fallen world, "normal" is broken and, as Christians, we are called to live as "peculiar people" (1 Peter 2:9 KJV). When our "normal" is unhealthy, we must be willing to be uncomfortable in order to pursue what God has for us.

We should expect that conflict done well will feel abnormal at first. This is even truer when we are being asked to live out a gospel truth that is so profoundly counterintuitive (losing your life in order to save it). As you wrestle with this discomfort, allow yourself to be challenged again by the phrase "the just shall live by faith" (Rom. 1:17 KJV; Gal. 3:11 KJV).

It will not be the skill with which you enact this gospel-laden conflict-drama that enriches your marriage. Instead, the faith you place in God to be better than the objects on the table will free you from the temptation to manipulate your spouse to appease your desires. This faith that "Christ is better" allows you to enjoy those desires as God intended.

Rest in the Gospel

Hopefully you can begin to hear in this approach to conflict something that reminds you of the sacraments of baptism and the Lord's Supper in its intent to provide a living picture or enactment of core gospel truths. To put it plainly, you should be able to set additional chairs at the table for your children or neighbors and share the gospel as you model it for them during conflict. (Note: you do not need to take this recommendation literally in order to soberly assess whether the gospel is impacting how you do conflict.)

Paul draws upon the gospel imagery of the sacrament of baptism in Romans 6:4: "We were buried therefore with him by baptism into death, in order that, just as Christ was raised from the dead by the glory of the Father, we too might walk in newness of life." Christians are to watch the process of baptism, remember our own conversion, and be encouraged. Non-Christians are invited to watch and learn about the gospel message as they see it lived out before their eyes.

The sacrament of the Lord's Supper is also meant to be a picture of the gospel as we ingest Christ's body and blood (represented by the bread and drink) to symbolize that we need Christ to transform us from the inside out and that only he is capable of sustaining our souls. Jesus is the bread that we eat to end our souls' hunger; the water we drink to cease our souls' thirst (John 4:10–14; 6:22–59; 7:37–39).

Christians regularly take the Lord's Supper to remind ourselves of who Christ is and what he has done so that we will not seek to satisfy our souls' hunger and thirst with any of the world's appealing but inadequate alternatives.

Similarly (although without the same biblical authority), we want to do conflict in a way that reminds us of core gospel truths and in a way that non-Christians could be drawn to the good news by watching. This is what it means to live gospel-centered lives so that our good works (both charitable actions and gracious self-control in difficult circumstances) shine before people and cause them to be drawn to our Father (Matt. 5:16).

What would this kind of evangelistic conversation sound like? Most of these conversations would come after a question from a friend who is dissatisfied with how he manages conflict. "How do you guys avoid the kinds of conflict I tell you about? How do you guys handle it when you disagree over things that are important to the two of you?"

With a quirky smile you could begin, "We have an odd way of reminding ourselves not to let the issue become more important than our marriage when it feels like our favorite things are at stake."

To which you would likely hear in reply, "Odd has got to be better than painful. If it works, I'd love to know what you do." From there you could walk him to both sides of the cross based upon this material—from Luke 9:23–24 to John 10:10: "The thief comes only to steal and kill and destroy. I [Jesus] came that they may have life and have it abundantly" (which is where we're going in "Take Three: Romance").

Jesus versus Satan

Before we transition to our third walk through Luke 9:23–24, let's contrast four points from John 10:10 with what we've been learning in order to set the stage for romance.

"Thief . . . Jesus". We will follow one of two agendas for our lives. There is the agenda of Satan in its many incarnations (which most often masquerade as our own broken "common sense"), all of which lead to our loss. There is one agenda of Jesus, which leads to life (Prov. 14:12; Matt. 7:13–14). Our choices, especially in the emotionally powerful moments of life, will be what ratify one of these two agendas.

"Steal . . . kill . . . destroy". If these words describe our post-conflict experiences—feeling robbed, depleted, and undone—then we can be certain that our approaches to conflict have been at odds with the gospel. That is more than saying that

we have broken the etiquette rules of Scripture (which is also true); it means that in the midst of our conflict we have tried to rely on God's blessings for what only God himself can provide (Jer. 2:11–13).

"Life". Here is that word from Luke 9:24 again. All Scripture is our Creator calling us back to the *life* he intended us to have. Like ignorant children we keep thinking that *life* will be found in our gifts from God rather than in our relationship with God—in the good things he provides for us rather than in the simple and transforming privilege of knowing him.

"Abundantly". God is not stingy, but he cannot extravagantly bless those who do not have his character—the Spirit of God bearing the fruit of love, joy, peace, patience, kindness, goodness, faithfulness, gentleness, and self-control in their souls (Gal. 5:22–23). In the absence of his character we become selfish with his abundance and create an atmosphere of competition and mistrust where there should be generosity and freedom. Apart from the transforming power of the gospel, even God's generosity cannot satisfy us enough to stop us from being suspicious and taking advantage of one another.

So we will see that romance is not a series of actions we add to our "marital to-do list" but an attitude of generosity and freedom toward our precious things—one that flows from the gospel and enables us to love our closest neighbors, our spouses, as ourselves (Matt. 22:39; Eph. 5:28–29). With that in mind, let's prepare to take a third narrative walk through our primary passage.

TAKE THREE: ROMANCE REIGNITED

Our temptation at this point is to think that we should rid the table of any desires besides Jesus. But with this attitude we would begin to feel awkwardly guilty for wanting the blessings of marriage or for having desires that come naturally with our personalities and passions. If we succumb to this way of thinking, change will be either short-lived or tainted by a martyr's tone.

We must apply the truth of Luke 9 to romance as well as we have applied it to conflict or we will have a love-hate relationship with our desires, making us fluctuate between guilt, anger, fear, and depression when they arise in our hearts and making marriage feel like a game we can never enjoy without being selfish idolaters.

Let's start by making two observations. First, the objects we fight over (those things still on the kitchen table) are the things we want in romance. There are not two lists—the things we are hurt by in conflict and the things we want in romance. They are the same list. This means that any book on marital conflict that does not continue on to romance is incomplete, and any book on romance that does not start with conflict is simplistic. The same heart with the same desires is active in both conflict and romance.

Second, after conflict, the things we wanted in romance become "weaponized." Once you've yelled at me about not being affectionate enough, it doesn't feel safe to come close to you anymore. After you've given me the cold shoulder for a week to passive-aggressively send the message that you wanted to spend more time together, coming close feels like a duty more than a delight.

Conflict changes both spouses' experience of the things on the kitchen table. For the person who wants them, they become so big that he is willing to sin to get them. For the person expected to give them, they become so powerful that they are seemingly unsafe to give ("What if I don't do it right? What if I can't speak that language? I'd be afraid to mess up with something that important and powerful").

This need not be the case if we draw the right conclusion from these two observations—that conflict done right can be very romantic. Conflict is the inevitable reality of two people sharing the same house, money, schedules, reputation, last name, and children. But conflict done well can be quite literally the best friend of a marriage.

Think of it this way. Anger says two things: (1) this is wrong and (2) it matters. Sinful anger says a third thing: (3) . . . more than you. When we do conflict poorly we add to the basket of things that are more important than our marriage, things we will gamble with setting the picture down in order to gain.

But in conflict done well, we are emptying the basket of things that are more important than our spouses. Instead of a growing list of unsafe subjects, there is a growing sense that we can go anywhere that is important to us in conversation and be safe. That is powerfully romantic, bordering on sexy.

Setting Another Table

Yes, I am "that counselor" who wants to take over your entire house, down to the decorations in your bedroom. Hopefully you're intrigued enough by what we've already covered that you'll continue with me. As before, even if you don't subscribe to the "Hambrickian School of Home Decorum," if you give yourself to the narrative that is being developed, it will change the way you see romance as much as it changed the way you do conflict.

Start by getting or repurposing an end table in your bedroom. For this exercise, cover it with a nice piece of fabric that matches the bedroom décor (so your spouse will let it stay in the room). At the back-center of the table place a tall, self-standing cross. It can be ornate or rustic—again, whichever will be allowed to stay in the bedroom.

In front of the cross place a framed edition of the same picture you hold during your kitchen-table conflicts. On one side of the table place your "objects of desire," and on the other side place your spouse's objects. You have set yourself up to do for your marriage what Jesus prescribed in Luke 9:23–24.

Each morning as you get ready for the day and each evening as you dress down, look at the table and be reminded of how God intends to bless your marriage through the gospel. The cross, which should be the tallest thing on the table, is central and gives meaning to everything else. Your desires are present but are there to serve God and your spouse.

Your mission is to refuse to be ruled by the things on your side of the table and to ensure that the objects on your spouse's side of the table never collect dust. A telltale sign of a gospel-centered marriage is when you spend more of your creative energy daydreaming about the things on your spouse's side of the table (Phil. 2:3–4).

Do couples really do this? Not naturally. Two things must be present for this to occur. First, you must believe that the gospel is satisfying even when your spouse is neglectful (which will still happen). Second, you need a consistent, tangible reminder of your spouse's desires or else your thoughts will drift back to your own.

How is this different from any other "Be nice" reminder system? Honestly, it can be used in the same moralistic manner. But the passage in which we are rooting this exercise, Luke 9:23–24, should remind us that the hope of a gospel-centered marriage is in God's promises, not our performances.

At this point you must realize that this is not a prescription for "how to always get it right in your marriage." Rather, this has been a lesson in how to root your difficult moments of conflict and powerful moments of romantic expectation in God's economy of grace rather than in our economy of need and entitlement.

God has always used these kinds of monuments and practices as ways to remind his people of his deliverance and promises in order to protect them from succumbing to idolatry again. The Jews celebrated Passover annually and had many other sacrifices and ceremonies. Christians take the Lord's Supper and observe baptism for the same reason.

God even told his people to decorate their homes in such a way that these truths would not be easily forgotten.

Hear, O Israel: The LORD our God, the LORD is one. You shall love the LORD your God with all your heart and with all your soul and with all your might. And these words that I command you today shall be on your heart. You shall teach them diligently to your children, and shall talk of them when you sit in your house, and when you walk by the way, and when you lie down, and when you rise. You shall bind them as a sign on your hand, and they shall be as frontlets between your eyes. You shall write them on the doorposts of your house and on your gates. (Deut. 6:4–9)

As you look at this table in your bedroom, realize that you are a primary means by which God intends to keep his promises to your spouse as she willingly "loses her life for his sake." You also play an important role in protecting your spouse from relying on his "objects of desire" more than on the gospel for life (Eph. 5:26).

Steady love that has a direct reminder of the gospel as its source is the best way to serve this protective role. You might even take a piece of paper to place under your spouse's "objects of desire" that says, "I am God's ambassador of protection for my spouse in these areas (2 Cor. 5:20)."

Chances are you will never have the opportunity to save your spouse from a violent intruder or an out-of-control vehicle—our odd, but common, mental images of "protecting our spouses." But you can daily cooperate with God to protect your spouse's soul from idolatry and bitterness by being skilled and creative in how you love your spouse.

Creativity with Direction

Hopefully now you can begin to see the things on your spouse's side of the table as blessings instead of burdens. Too often, after a marriage event, we leave with the weight of a long "to-do list." If the event was "really practical" we have clear guidelines about how frequently we're to do them (e.g., one date per week, sex 2.5 times per week, and compliments seven times for any negative comment). But prescribed kindness loses the life that makes it romantic.

The beauty of gospel-centered romance is that it allows your spouse to add new desires to the table without your having a defensive reaction—"Great! More things for me to do. More things I won't do to suit you. Another bar I will never be able to reach. Another foreign love language for me to learn. My spouse thinks I'm the Rosetta Stone of romance when I'm really Hooked on Phonics." This freedom to express desire without creating pressure is the key to growing a marriage of romance.

Marriage "ruts" are the inevitable outcome of not expressing new desires or being creative with old ones. Over a lifetime you and your spouse will change in profound ways. This necessitates a great deal of learning, sharing, and creativity or your romantic efforts will quickly become mundane, routine, and out of date.

Every marriage needs a system of communication that allows new desires to enter the conversation without a building sense of pressure or defensiveness. Every spouse should be asking both "How can I use my spouse's longstanding desires to romance him in this season of life?" and "What things are becoming more important to my spouse that I can use to bless her?"

Until this happens, romance will be a pressure to avoid rather than a blessing in which to engage. So invite your spouse to add things to his or her side of the table in order to give you more food for thought about how you can fulfill God's promise to give your spouse what he or she enjoys ("life") abundantly.

Take joy in being the hand and voice of God in the life of the person you love most. Allow this to become a significant portion of your life calling and your most enjoyable hobby. As you do, you will find that God is fulfilling his promise to you at the same time. As you "lose your life for his sake" to bless your spouse, undoubtedly you will discover that you have found the "life" (enjoyment) you thought you were sacrificing.

FOUR QUESTIONS

As you seek to assimilate what you've learned in this material, here are four questions you need to consider. Taking the time to review these questions will help you to walk away with more than just a couple of new tools for your toolbox, which will quickly be discarded and forgotten if that is all you take away. Instead, use these questions to solidify a paradigm that allows the gospel to (almost literally) transform conflict into foreplay.

First, have you given your life to Christ by forsaking your driving desires in favor of his grace? If not, everything that we have said is unattainable. Jesus will not be reduced to a technique. We do not add his ideas to our lives in order to try them out and see if we like them best. We do not get to date Jesus. Until we are his, he is not ours (and neither are his blessings).

This first question is much bigger than saying, "Do you understand the principles and applications that we've discussed?" You can understand it well enough to teach it—with even better clarity, humor, and case examples than this booklet provides—and yet not have access to the power that makes the message effective (2 Tim. 3:5).

Jesus did not come to remedy our lack of understanding. There have always been great teachers. Jesus came to remedy the problem of our selfish, foolish hearts. Jesus is not content to be merely our teacher; that is a role inadequate to meet our real need. Jesus demands to be our Lord.

> We never have followed the advice of the great teachers. Why are we likely to begin now? Why are we more likely to follow Christ than any of the others? Because He is the best moral teacher? But that makes it even less likely that we shall follow Him. If we cannot take the elementary lessons, is it likely we are going to take the most advanced ones? If Christianity only means one more bit of good advice, then Christianity is of no importance. There has been no lack of

good advice for the last four thousand years. A bit more will make no difference.[1]

Second, what have you considered "life" and refused to place, both once for all and daily, at the foot of the cross? It is the things we try to rescue from the cross that become our self-inflicted prisons. If our embrace of the gospel is going to be more than a point-in-time decision (and it must be more, if Christ is our Lord), then this is the most important question of daily gospel living.

The answer to this second question involves more than marital conflict and romance. Answering this question is the key to emotional health (e.g., dealing with anxiety, depression, anger, and so on), avoiding a midlife crisis, balanced parenting, having a healthy relationship with food, and not being consumed by your work.

> If suffering alone taught, all the world would be wise, since everyone suffers. To suffering must be added mourning, understanding, patience, love, openness, and the willingness to remain vulnerable. . . .
>
> Communication is thus the blood of marriage that carries vital oxygen into the heart of our romance. . . .
>
> Marriage provides the small experimental laboratory whereby we can learn to engage in spiritual fellowship. Everything that happens broadly in social contexts has a mirror in marriage—disagreements, wounding words, conflict of interests, and competing dreams.[2]

This simply echoes what Jesus' little brother said: "For we all stumble in many ways. And if anyone does not stumble in what he says, he is a perfect man, able also to bridle his whole body"

1. C. S. Lewis, *Mere Christianity* (1952; repr. New York: HarperCollins, 2001), 156.
2. Gary Thomas, *Sacred Marriage* (Grand Rapids: Zondervan, 2000), 143, 158, 162.

(James 3:2). Conflict and romance are about taming the tongue, but marriage is where our tongue feels most free. If we can tame the organ most closely connected to our hearts (Luke 6:45) in the environment where we feel most free, then the gospel is permeating the depths of our souls.

Third, how do you seek to "save your life" in conflict (e.g., what are your specific behavior patterns or verbal tactics)? We often want to explain our actions in conflict as mere reactions to our spouses. But Scripture does not call these "innocent reactions." Instead, Scripture calls this "the flesh" and says it must be put to death: "For if you live according to the flesh you will die, but if by the Spirit you put to death the deeds of the body, you will live" (Rom. 8:13).

When we call these actions "reactions to our needs being unmet" or "aspects of our personality to be accepted," we cut ourselves off from the power of the gospel. Neither rudeness nor any other form of unhealthy communication is a personality type. The cycle of explaining bad behavior by bad behavior is a slippery slope from which Christ rescued us at the cost of his blood.

In light of this, our call is to eliminate the life-seeking (but death-creating) patterns we fall into as we serve our overgrown desires. This is a vital step for establishing peace and laying the foundation for romance. It is at this point that the lordship of Jesus becomes so personal that it begins to revolutionize your closest relationship—marriage.

Fourth, do you truly believe that God will keep his promise to give you life if you sacrifice what you consider to be life for his sake? This belief is essential because the transformation of your marriage will follow the same pattern as the transformation of your life—up and down, times of struggle and times of success.

Unless we truly believe this promise, we will quit when times get hard and will grow bitter over the things we lost when we "tried things God's way." This is why living out the gospel requires more community than your marriage can provide.

Faith—holding on to God's promises during hard times—was never meant to be an individual sport, or even a two-player game. Faith is always a community project.

If you are serious about doing the things we've talked about, it will involve more than sitting at the kitchen table and redecorating your bedroom; it will also involve inviting people into your living room. If you allow other couples whom you and your spouse trust to know how you're applying this material, your likelihood of continuing to apply the material after the first time it "doesn't work" will increase exponentially.

While it may seem off subject at first, a final word needs to be said. Sermons, seminars, conferences, and books don't change marriages. Plenty of messages have been heard and pages read without marital enrichment occurring. Even counseling is not the most effective means of marital enrichment. Counseling, while it can be helpful, is short-term and artificial.

I have heard too many people say, "We read the best books, went to the best events, dated each other regularly, and still had our marriage go sour." But although I would recommend all those activities, I have never heard a couple say, "We have been honest with mutually trusted friends about our struggles in each season of life, and have received prayer and biblical guidance, but our marriage still went bad."

What changes marriage over the long term is the gospel lived out in gospel community. What you have here is the gospel *content* to discuss in gospel *community*. If you live out God's Word in the context of God's people, then you will experience what God intended marriage to be.

> "Therefore a man shall leave his father and mother and hold fast to his wife, and the two shall become one flesh." This mystery is profound, and I am saying that it refers to Christ and the church.
> (Eph. 5:31–32)